PRAI**

WISDOM TEETH

"We need more songs like this young man's right here. Truth cuts its way beneath the unspoken like new teeth on their way to light. Son of Langston, come on through."
   —Ruth Forman, author of *Prayers Like Shoes*

"Full of wit and whimsy, *Wisdom Teeth* postulates a poetics of heart-whole appreciation and honesty—for love and life, for family and friends, for literature and history, for pop culture and the poet's ever-cognizant powers of observation."
   —Tony Medina, author of *My Old Man
   Was Always on the Lam*

"Derrick Weston Brown ventures into the canon to echo the voices of Morrison's Sweet Home Men, then bends his ear to the streets of D.C. to render the shouts and whispers of corner brawls and slapped down dominoes—all the while balancing the bridge between Ellington and the sacred tribes of hip-hop."
   —Tyehimba Jess, author of *Leadbelly*

Wisdom Teeth

Poems by
Derrick Weston Brown

Wisdom Teeth
Derrick Weston Brown © 2011

ISBN: 978-1-60486-417-5
LCCN: 2010916476

Busboys and Poets Press
2121 14th St. NW
Washington, DC 20009
www.busboysandpoets.com

PM Press
P.O. Box 23912
Oakland, CA 94623
pmpress.org

Printed in the USA on recycled paper.

Layout: Jonathan Rowland

TABLE OF CONTENTS

Wisdom Teeth

Ajar

Notes

About the Author

Acknowledgements

This moment has been brought to you by the encouragement, guidance, and prayers of many. I feel your hands pressed to my back, constantly pushing me forward even when I drag my feet. To all of you, named and unnamed, thank you.

Mighty thanks to the many centers of learning and institutions of higher education for providing space, resources, and refuge, without which, the birthing of this book would not have happened: American University's Creative Writing Program, Cave Canem Foundation and Summer Retreat, D.C. Creative Writing Workshop, Hart Middle School, Howard University and The Funky Cold Workshop, Haiku North America Conference, Hurston-Wright Foundation, Lannan Foundation, The Squaw Valley Community of Writers, and VONA.

First of all, I must thank my Mom, Rita Brown, my first teacher, publisher, voice of constant encouragement, and corner woman, who pushed me back out there to fight mediocrity in my work and in my life, when I wanted to quit out of frustration and laziness, and when things got difficult. Thanks to my Dad, Bernard Brown Jr., who unknowingly set me on the poets' path when he gave me an illustrated book of poems entitled *My Daddy Is a Cool Dude* by Karama Fufuka. I also have to thank my immediate and extended family, Nana, Monet, and Alicia for encouraging me unflinchingly, to keep reading and keep writing and never abandon my imagination or my dreams and determination. I love y'all!

Super mighty love and gratitude to Andy Shallal, the founder of Busboys and Poets, Busboys and Poets Press, and the foundation of which so many things are being built upon. If you had told me that this was possible five years ago as I began selling books and trying to establish poetry programming worthy of the U St. and Washington, D.C.'s rich poetry legacy, I wouldn't have believed you. What a journey! Thank you for your trust, and your heart, and imagination. What a book cover! What's next?

Pamela Pinnock! Our friendship starts way before Busboys and Poets was even an idea. I have no idea how to express my thanks for your encouragement and constant belief in my poetry, my attributes, and for championing me in public and private. I see pride in your eyes every time we talk, hug, or share a kind word in passing. You are, in Langston's words, my Dreamkeeper. Thank you. This book is, because you are.

Big thanks to Craig O'Hara at PM Press! You are a study in patience and clear-cut no-nonsense innovation. Thank you for providing a stable and independent home for not only my book, but for all the books that PM Press both publishes and distributes. Thank you for founding and maintaining one of the strongest independent publishers out there, and thank you for the education.

Don Allen. I may not say it much, but rest assured that I appreciate everything you've done for me. You are the one who really put all of this into action. You are the reason why I work at Busboys and Poets as both a seller of books and as a Poet-In-Residence. Thank you for the opportunities you've provided and the invaluable knowledge you've given me for nearly ten years. There's so much more I could say, but I'm running out of words, and room.

Thank you! Teaching For Change! The best nonprofit I've ever worked for and whose mission, I am honored to say, I have tried to uphold through my work as a book seller. Big thanks to executive director, Deborah Menkart, Jennifer Wolfe, Jennifer Arrington, Katie Seitz, and the rest of the wonderful staff.

Much gratitude to all of my teachers and mentors: Cornelius Eady, Ruth Forman, Keith Leonard, E. Ethelbert Miller, Laini Mataka, Tony "The Funky Cold" Medina, Myra Sklarew, Bro. Yao, Sonia Sanchez, Henry Taylor, and all the great faculty at Cave Canem, Squaw Valley, and VONA.

Finally, I have to take a deep breath to thank the following folks, friends, colleagues, fellow poets, and all around good people, who helped me get here, to this very moment. So in no particular order, here goes… Alan King (my best friend and brother-in-arms), Fred Joiner (my main man), Jati Lindsay, Truth Thomas, Denise Johnson, Ebony Golden, Simone Jacobson, Marlene Hawthrone-Thomas (the best photographer ever), Nijla Mumin, Kali Ferguson, Tara Betts, Ernesto Mercer, Brandon Johnson, Gary Lilley, Brian Gilmore, Face, Patrick Washington, John Murillo, Bianca Spriggs, Johnathan Moody, Venus Thrash, Reginald Dwayne Betts, Kyle Dargan, Holly Bass, Jenny Lares, Sarah Browning, Kimberly Washington, Abdul Ali, Adia Blackmon Shabazz, Ekoko Omadeke, Tim Seibles, Marita Golden, Tinesha Davis, Evie Shockley Tyehimba Jess, A. Van Jordan, Katy Ritchey, Nicole Sealy, Jennifer Steele, Melanie Henderson, Myisha Cherry, Tazuo Yamaguchi, Sandra Beasley, Tala A. Rameh, Aracelis Girmay, Tim'm West, Ruth Ellen Kocher, De'Lana Dameron, Adrian Matejka, Randall Horton, Regie Cabico, Beny Blaq, Thomas Sayers Ellis, Tayari Jones, Reginald Harris, Adrian Ayers, Deheija Maat, Terri Cross-Davis, Hayes Davis, Dr. Jeffery Leake, Nikky

Finney, Sonya Renee, Darry Strickland, Douglass Kearney, Linda Susan Jackson (Playa!), Patricia Spears Jones, Kenny Tanemura, Evie Shockley, Ashaki Jackson, Nancy Schwalb, Bassey Ikpi, Remica Bingham-Risher, Nicki Miller, Cedric Tillman, Amanda Johnson, Kim Roberts, Henry Taylor and all of my Cave Canem, Mangoes, Original Mocha Hut, VONA, American University family. To anyone I may have missed, you are among these pages in spirit, if not in name. Thank you.

G rateful acknowledgement is also made to the editors of the following publications in which these poems appear, sometimes in different versions:

Amistad: "Paul A to Paul D Eintou," "Paul A Stumps Schoolteacher Eintou," "Paul A and the Rake Tooth"

Beltway Poetry Quarterly: "Missed Train," "Ol' Man Strength," "Thirty Mile Woman: Sixo's Song"

Cave Canem Tenth Anniversary Anthology: Gathering Ground: "Thirty Mile Woman: Sixo's Song"

Borderline: "Halle Tells How They Broke Him"

Columbia Poetry Review: "What I'm Told: Paul D's Origin"

Drunken Boat online journal: "Snagglepuss Spills His Guts on *E! True Hollywood Story*"

Full Moon on K Street: Poems About Washington, D.C.: "Missed Train"

Ginosko Literary Journal: "Mirrored Eintou"

LocusPoint online journal: "Building," "Remembering Bonita Applebum," "Hourglass Flow," "Till's Skin," "Slow Fade"

MiPOesias online magazine: "Paul A's Eintou," "Red Giant," "White Dwarf"

Mythium: The Journal of Contemporary Literature and Cultural Voices: "To Be Published"

Un-Mute online literary magazine: "Poem about running into you on the street after not seeing you for a while."

Words. Beats. Life. journal: "Misdirected," "Remembering Bonita Applebum"

Foreword
My Words Of Wisdom

Derrick Weston Brown has been sharing poems with me, bravely opening himself up to my critical responses, for close to six years now. I have been privileged to follow the trajectory of his writing career and the disciplined refinement of his craft, both of which are evident in his first collection of poems, *Wisdom Teeth*. This brilliant first effort is akin to a mixtape, filled with nostalgic hip-hop references—MF Doom, A Tribe Called Quest, and J Dilla, among others—a love letter from a grown man still much enamored of the youth culture today. Found here are playful experiments with the eintou, bop, and brownku, African American forms seldom approached with such mastery.

There is a quintessentially *D.C.* (dee-cee) quality to these poems. We cannot call it Washington, as that would diminish the urban lifeline coursing through the work. Familiar neighborhoods and community hubs—K Street, Adams Morgan, U Street—and references to specifics like area codes might be lost on those outside the so-called Diamond District, but will be undoubtedly cherished by locals. The "down home" blues, soul, and R&B music in Derrick's work is reinforced by his marriage of urban and country worlds. The idea of home is reconstructed with each stroke of the pen, bonding the reader to disparate environments with the ease of a man well-traveled and easily likable. The poet code-switches in at least 10 different vernaculars, all believable and authentic. Here, we find the lover, here, the scholar, and later, the "practicing" Buddhist.

Wisdom Teeth offers a collective biography of the complexity of Black male existence in America. In "The Sweet Home Men Series," Brown shows a different brand of masculinity, one where men long for a woman's touch and presence, for freedom, for affection. The series brings to light themes of manhood, brotherhood, delicacy, warmth among men, love for other men, love for women. But it's Paul D who reveals the essence of what the poet is aiming to express:

> *You'd think I'd have*
> *A whole mess of tears shed by now.*

Brown's characters (and autobiographical poems) allow us to see their calloused, imperfect selves, as well as a tenderness absent from much literature pertaining to Black masculinity. He brings to the page an old skool chivalry, complemented with perfect word packages like "yawn of ruin," which are never contrived. We're reminded of the familiar plague of the "good guy gift," and faced with questions of manhood not easily answered. In places, the poems border on woman worship. But, one can quickly recognize the inner riot of the heart, admiring from afar, trying to find the right approach.

Derrick's candid portrait of Black male identity exposes vulnerability as plainly as turning over a palm to feel its softer side, especially in poems like "Building" and "Kitchen Gods" where the poet is at his finest. These are men you know, men whose layers are seldom shown as frankly. These men are complex, gentle, brotherly, and strong. They muse about their own fears and social pressures, and then accept

> *I am a man and a slave to*
> *the general understanding that*
> *we must make the first move.*

At times, the work is wickedly funny and irreverent, too. Some titles are almost as long as the poems themselves because the poetry has the effortless quality of coffee shop conversation. Derrick is sitting right next to you, making perfect literary doodles on your bar nap. *Wisdom Teeth* swings with ease between youth and adulthood, history and the present. In the age of Twitter and Four Square, these poems answer the question "Where ya at?" with specific places, moments, feelings, smells, sounds, and snapshots of history. The work is intensely personal, and so we're privy to missed opportunities between lovers and friends, learning in sync with the author that missteps along the journey are inevitable. And, in "Sourpatch Kiss," the poet keeps it real:

> *I think what I want*
> *is a plain poem that*
> *doesn't come off as*
> *pleading prose*

Indeed, the poet has succeeded. It's truly extraordinary that it has taken this long for Derrick's collection to be published, but his contributions to the greater literary community in D.C. are not without merit. I have been fortunate to catch glimpses of the experiences that went into the crafting of these poems, on the many occasions I found myself at the bookstore on 14th and V Streets NW. *Wisdom Teeth* indicates the stubborn release of the past, the things we choose to let go and the things that make our men ache with pain. The gentle discomfort that has been nudging the poet's craw under the surface finally comes to light on these pages. I urge you to find value in the simple pleasure of these poems as you read them.

Simone Jacobson
June 26, 2010
Washington, D.C.

Hourglass Flow

Hourglass Flow

"To write all night long, the hourglass is still slow
flow from Hellborn to free power like Wilco." —MF Doom, MC

Blame comfort. Blame a city of coffee houses and lounges.
Blame ego and pride and all that clever shit. Blame self.

Blame the crafty inner only child and his addiction to pleasing
and head pats. Blame the anxious inner prospector and gold fever.

Blame the voice that wants to sound like a poet, but not sound
like a poet wanting to sound like a poet. Blame distractions

but again that brings it all back to self doesn't it? Blame ritual.
Blame fear of failure. Blame the voice in your head that doesn't like you.

Blame competition. Blame loathing and book deal envy. Blame the workshop
in your head. Blame expectations the size of a pig iron plow.

Blame clock faces and hour hands. Blame stuck keys and humming hard drives.
Blame that lost hour of slumber. Blame unreadable REM sleep scribble.

Then

Remember the ritual of trying, falling, the get up and dust off.
The look to see if anyone is watching. The start over. The hopeful ending.

Remember each day is a draft. Remember possibility. Process.
Remember place. Remember voice. Patience. Remember to forgive
yourself.

Write.

The Sweet Home Men Series

For Toni Morrison

Thirty Mile Woman: Sixo's Song

I ask
the wind for
guidance. In
this place
the trees know me now
Earth is still earth
and Black-eyed-susans
do not differ
so much
from African
violets.
They want me to speak
the tubob talk.
Stop
the dancing,
so I may not
find myself.
When I am lost you find me.
Gather me
when I am pieces.
Gather me.   Love

the pieces that
I am.
Give me back to me
in all the right
order,
friend of my mind.
I have
asked permission
of all creation
to let us meet.
Time is your
hard breath
in the field.
I move
when the wind
wills it.
We have tomorrow and
today.
Thirty mile woman,
meet me at the crossroads.

All He Can

Paul A Speaks on Sethe

I mean
We men ain't we?
She the first ripe woman we seen
in years.
But she the only one.
One.
She the one that got to choose.
We brothers. Right?
Men.
Sweet Home men.
Mr. Garner say so.
We make our own decisions.
Pick and choose.
Wake when we wanna.
Work when we wanna.
But this girl. I'm so sick with want.
Need.
When I see her I can taste the honeysuckle on her neck.
I am the maker.
Paul D is the tiller.
Paul F is the thinker
And Sixo just African as he wanna be.
Halle got a mama. So he at least know a woman.
I cut a glance at this girl. This Sethe
with her iron eyes.
My heart get full.
My legs get heavy.
Between them is a churn

thick with urgency.
I am the maker.
Conjure hands.
She leave me useless.
Can't build nothing.
This girl messing with me.
I dream of parting
comeandgo
comeandgo.
Lawd. We agreed to wait.
Let her choose. But
the urge.
We men right?
Men fucking suckling calves.
Lawd I can't take much more of this.
I need to know.
My hands good for only
two things.
She choose me
maybe three.
Tell me.
Tell me this one thing.
How much is a nigger supposed to take?
Tell me.
How much?

Sethe's Haiku for a Sweet Home Man

It was his hands   yeah
His hands givin hands lovin hands
That's why I choose him.

Paul D's Haiku for Sethe

I always loved trees
Long thick limbs swaying brown boughs
Sethe   be my Oak.

What I'm Told: Paul D's Origin

They say when I come along
I was the youngest.
Last.

When I come, they say
my momma burst into
tears at the sight of me.
Couldn't stop.

I remember drops feeling
like tiny wet fingertips
on my face. So I knew rain.
Early.

The old woman who
pulled me slick and quiet from between
my momma's thighs said I
was born with a veil on my face.

Said it was the sign of the charmed.
Who ever bear it is a seer.
Can look into the before
the could be and the soon come.

But my veil not the
kind that calls for fortune
or the color of that
great get up morning sun.

My veil the color
of a work hoe. Dull.
Cloudy day gray.

So I reckon as it is so
My life supposed to be
hard.
I reckon.

My coming filled with tears.
Maybe my going be the same.

But the damndest thing.

My gift.
Momma told me I
was special. Blessed even.
But every woman I come close to
weep and moan.

Some holler hold me tight
and tremble like a chill
done wrapped itself around
every bone in they body and
seeped through to settle in the marrow.

Some just twist
they self up like a cloth
fat with rain and squeeze
out every last tear.

They bosom heaving like
the blacksmith's billows
do when he fashioning
shoes for a mare.

I don't shed many tears
myself. Though I reckon I
got cause to.

They sold momma around
my twelfth year.
My friends dead.
Sold.

Then I find myself
on the block.
White hands all in my mouth
tugging my ears.

Fingers all up and around
my never mind.

Then I end up here.
At Sweet Home.
Me. The newest Paul
soon to be the last.

You'd think I'd have
A whole mess of tears shed by now.

No.
I stored my
heart away where it couldn't
never be touched. I keep it
buried in the dark of me

where it can beat dry and quiet.
Free from all that salty love
leaking from women's eyes.

When I come around
they tongue confess.

They hearts empty out
onto their faces and for a moment
they turn loose of they pain.

Some gift. Some blessing.

I'm charmed.

That's what I'm told.

Paul A to Paul D Eintou

Brother
Before we run
In case we caught and strung
Know we as free as Brother Tree
Our roots watered somewhere
In earth that love
Lord know

Paul A Stumps Schoolteacher Eintou

What you
get when you treat
a man like a prized pig?
Force him to root, rut, grunt, squeal, dig
You smart   study his eyes
What you see there?
Don't know?

Paul A and the Rake Tooth

I heard
school teachers like
fresh apples before class
Ain't got no apple just this tooth
Bone straight rust brown so sharp
My treat

Halle Tells How They Broke Him

"Let me tell you something. A man ain't a goddamn ax…
Chopping busting every goddamn minute of the day!
Things get to him. Things he can't chop down because
they're inside!" —Paul D

I.

Churn

Churn

My brains is soured
all the rich gone.

What is left
that they ain't already taken?

Think you got say-so
they break they neck to prove

different. Prayer ain't mine
either. Money never been mine.

Best I ever did besides
Sethe and the babies was

working my fingers to
the gristle to buy my own mama
a clear path.

II.

Curdle

Curdle

When things get thick
you add milk
to get the thin

Add milk for righteous biscuits

Sweet cream to the cornmeal

Add milk to cull the heat out a burn

Milk is life and

they took
they took
they took.

Call me anything but a Man.

What is a man if his hands can't
hold on to something
build something
plant chop cook crop kill reap?

Man ain't suppose to hide,
to thief, steal away.

A man supposed to do.

What you do when they
cut your hands off with no knife?

What you do when they
steal the run in your legs?

Sixo say we made of things
stronger than what fills they
skins.

But where they learn
how to break us in places
we can't see?

Wrap our song up in
their fists then beat us with it?

III.

Its like they know
when you get close
to heaven and they
smell it and they move
they see the dance in
your eyes and they
read it word for word
they smell the sweet
and they want it for them
selves and they ease in

like air like a corn snake
and they snatch it and rip
it open like they did my
Sethe's shirt and cut
a chokecherry tree
on her oak brown back
with a beast's skin flayed
and worn and wicked
and them boys
them mossy teeth boys
rolled her on her back
suckled like two pale piglets
and their grunts
turned my brains
to porridge and I
couldn't do nothing
couldn't cry out
cause they don't
deserve to hear my
pain that's for Sethe
only only she didn't
make a sound but her
eyes was searching
wet and wide and
those eyes went
back to iron and
I wanted
I wanted
to make
a trench
of their heads

with a shovel
but my spine
is butter

my heart has curdled
my brain is clabber
and my babies have no
milk and I can't run
with no spine
where can I go
where they can't take
my babies milk or
me or mama cause
they took my mind when
they took Sethe
and I saw
I saw I saw I saw
and the sour got in me
and stayed and
call me anything but
a man.

IV.

This is where my mind
smeared thick and sticky
churned and curdled
call me anything
call me anything
but.

The Unscene

Duke Ellington's You St. Lament

I try to follow his eyes
see where his stare lands.

The Duke watches from an elevated
perch. Now.

Not like before
when his face used to be
ground level.

Maybe he just
watches over you, me and the
faces still left
in the color
corridor.

Or maybe that's a
worried look
on his wrinkled brow

as if he's dreading
a gentrified tap
on his shoulder
reminding even the Duke
to fear a rise in rent.

Missed Train

I smelled you at the Metro stop
Tasted you on the Yellow
Glimpsed you on the Green
Caught you on the Orange
Loved you on the Red
Lost you on the Blue

Now I need a transfer
or at least exit fare,
cause no one deserves
to take such a ride
and end up taken
for every dime

Baby
You a last minute change of plans
an unexpected call at the God hour
that leaves me feeling mortal.

Mirrored Eintou

Teddy Roosevelt Island
Washington D.C.

I.
stunning
a black man leaf
my skin's shade lies within
takes to air a sunspot halo
leaves hued gold yellow green
fistful of fall
lone bridge

II.
lone bridge
fistful of fall
leaves hued gold yellow green
takes to air a sunspot halo
my skin's shade lies within
a black man leaf
stunning

Anacostia Eintou

Taste the
Sweet outer crust
Baked brown brick road newness
Mississippi crossroad cleaved cake
Anacostia core
Fading chocolate
city

While watching a sister's rear end mow through my field of vision and inspire a poem.

Friday, September 30, 2005, late afternoon

Call it sweet swing music hidden in
the back of a denim pendulum
east westin down "you" street
on a Friday half past rush hour

Color Commentary

We step out of Tryst,
onto the Adams Morgan
streets and into Thursday
night fights.

The stoop of the storefront
pizza shop is a beehive,
a sound clash of words
colors, smells.
Garlic competes with
Cool Water, liquor
sweat, and close quarters club funk.
We watch this soup bubble
burst.

Young brother in an Iceberg
t-shirt and jeans
gets into it with a beefy Italian cat.

Onlookers drag their feet
circle up
becoming turkey vultures
their necks craning.

A lanky brother breaks the circle
reasoning with Iceberg Slim.
Nah son. Fuck em.
Let's roll to Timheri's
-plenty youngin's at Timheri's.

Beef-a-Roni wastes no time.
Let's the word
faggot fly

a clay pigeon hurled
into the dimension of
no-take backs.

There's a Greek chorus of
Ooohs.

Iceberg's jaws tighten,
Nah. Fuck that shit Hol' my pizza.

Beefy does the same.
Leaving his slice of pie
in the hands of a buddy
waiting.

Iceberg still talking
pulls off his shirt
tosses it to Mr. Peacemaker
launches a wide arcing swing.
Beefaroni pauses
readies himself
and spills into Iceberg like
paint.

They are Cervantes's windmills
on concrete.

Their arms are Jackson Pollock
brush strokes.

Iceberg is an erupting bass line
stuttered by Beefy's
Timberland beat patterns.

Iceberg grabs a
handful of shirt
guards his head
No matter.

Beefy's fists
dig through his ribs
like topsoil.

We watch disappointed.
It's Rocky and Apollo Creed
all over again.
Represent for the brothers!
someone yells but the ten count
is on and Iceberg can't hear over
Beefaroni beating his djembe body.

A bouncer from a club
nearby pulls them apart.

Beefy springs up huffing.
His eyes are strobes dancing
around the circle of brothers

his smirk an invitation for more.
He grabs his pizza strolls
down the block. Maybe later he'll cool
his stinging knuckles with the
victory beer his buddies will buy him.

Iceberg is led away by his crew
who pelt him with hailstone insults.

Bring your bitch-ass on

-let that white boy beat you

-tha fuck!?

I feel cheated, says Yao.

He definitely ain't from this area
Alan reasons, *we'd a stole him*
off top. No talking.

Did you see that dip spin move
white-boy put on that dude?

The laughter a tremor in Fred's
body, *Yo that was classic.*

Around us post-fight analyses
commence. Onlookers morph into

Larry Merchant and George Foreman,
comparing fight stats, punches thrown,
landed.

We disperse
disappointed at the under card
not quite ready
for the main event.

Building

For Fred Joiner, Jati Lindsay, and Dominoes

A syrup of sunlight coats
the hard table

where they lay hands
on dry bones

glossy bones

steady trash talk and chuckles
season the snap crack

of spotted flat backs
as point are claimed

Five!
    Ten!
Twenty!

Fingers drum the table.

I'm on my third house.
Where you at!? Jati?
HUD is officially
in the building!

A flat palmed rim shot retort
shakes the table.

The bones shiver loose
like unhinged teeth.

Tight lipped plotting
dreadlocks brush the bones

Jati resets the fracture
smiling as houses change ownership

Eminent domain Fred!
You getting gentrified!

Shoulders hold the rupture of
laughter.

Yo! Who's stirring the soup
now Fred?

The bones rustle.
A field of pale on burgundy table top.

Brown hands reach in
for another claiming.

K St. Lunch Hour Tanka

Hands ache to eclipse
the full of an Autumn moon
conjoined Jupiters
I churn and swell   a blue tide
that laps against your curved shore

Brownku

Malcolm X Park D.C.
April 26, 2009

Long limbed dancer sways
body sheathed in sweat and sun
butterscotch churned wombman

Mother to Son

(Overheard in a 14th St. Bookstore)

Boy,
I'm trying to buy you
these books!

Your Grandma's trying to buy you these
books as a gift. For free!

And you gonna cry!?

Cause we won't get you the
book you want!?

Mom, you see this?

Mmm hmmm

Boy you better stop crying and whinin!

I didn't raise you to be suburban!!!!

Now dry it up!

What It's Like to Date in D.C. for Those Who Haven't.

After Patricia Smith
For Roshani Kothari

It's like having a mouthful of prayers
when all you looking for is that one
Amen.

Kitchen Gods

After the poets photo by Mignonette E. Dooley

we lean on kitchen counter tops
like pool sticks
swirling spirits in
plastic cups.

mouths full of laughter
as we blow the dust off

old stories like records
that hadn't seen a turntable
in some time.

we resuscitate the
ghosts of old lovers
angry indifferent or otherwise.

don't miss a beat
as we solo
and lasso loop words   finish

each other's sentences
scarf down bowls of
red beans rice

chase em with
rum that
warms the gullet

makes gut chuckles flow
easy.
we hold our sides

feign kidney aches
kick out legs
as memory plays marionette

we lean cool   shoulder to shoulder
like blue-black ridge
mountain ranges

our hands map out
a woman's dimensions   mold
hips out of thin air
recreating
her walk and
arching calves

we connect
the dots
that bring hearsay

to hear-to-fore
hereafter
truth-truth

swear to god   co-sign
my man is right here
he'll verify

we shoo the little
ones out of the kitchen
with gentle hands

pausing when the language
gets a little cerulean
with g'dams and g'lords

we dap
bump fists so hard
rings skip sparks

and concur with
a meeting of
plastic cup rims

we a small kitchen crew
salt and pepper gray
mixed with adinkra symbols,

skin the color
of smoked chestnut
smelling like our fathers.

our mother's milk
distant memories
on our breath

we grown

we hoppin-john
lavender sage
a lone hand slapping go-go on skins

we earmen
we eight deep
standing on kitchen tile

a blood knot
of the quick
tongued   with quicker pens

202
301
240
poets.

Wisdom Teeth

Legacy

My father's vocabulary
is extensive but
he still can't find the words
for I love you.

Nor the synonyms
acronyms
or abbreviations.

I guess this is why I am
a poet.

I inherited the words
lost to his dictionary.

I am the new volume.

Updated.

New testament.

Forgiveness Poem

After Randall Horton

Alicia Turnbull
didn't do anything
but breathe and be a girl.

It was her skin we didn't like.
This was back then when to
be dark was to be a punch line

-Hey Licia! *you so black*
when they called your
name at night school and
you said here they still marked
you absent!

-Hey Licia! *You so black*
you leave finger prints
on charcoal.

Alicia Turnbull didn't do
nothing but be. Be a
girl, be a sister, be the
darkest child in her family,
in her class, in after-school.

We tore her down daily.
What a smile.
We smashed it.
What a laugh.

We choked it.

She cried every day.
Fought the older girls
who called her names
smacked her upside
the head and claimed
they still couldn't
knock the Black off.

I was the nice one
but I pitched in too
the day she tried to sit
next to me at the swimming pool.

My friends started hollering
and I turned to her and said

*Don't nobody want to sit
by your ol' ugly black self.*

Alicia Turnbull
didn't do anything but
breathe, be a girl, a sister,
a daughter.

We made her a shadow.
Stole her light till she
disappeared.

Forgive me Alicia
for not seeing
your beauty
and believing
the perm kit,
TV, fading cream
whispers that
said our brown,
cocoa, red tinged,
black berry hues were
injury to insult.

Forgive me for believing
that night held no glory to day.
Forgive me for holding
white washed fairy tales
as truth.

Forgive my ugliness
and my dark heart.
Where ever you are
forgive me.

Gust

1989 Charlotte, North Carolina, Hurricane Hugo

The sky snarled.
We heard God swallow cumulus,
stratus, and anvil headed nimbus
before the hush.

We ventured outside
peered up into the calm.
The sky   a frosted snow globe
swirl of stars.

The moon
a glossy clear polished
fingernail sliver
winked.

Odd
The wind so strong
I could lean into it
arms out and not fall.
I was Pisa.

What did I know
of nature's way
of teaching lessons?

That there is
an eye of the storm.

Watch me smile.

My back to the rifle
sight of lassoed menace
clueless to the coming stretch
and yawn of ruin.

Till's Skin

Lesson #1

I.
Second to last summer
before high school
me and Brooke Petty were
a neighborhood item.

Sugar water lovers.
Ten speed bike sunset rendezvous
at a creek bed.

Here we would trade spearmint kisses
and work the squeeze play
between first and second base.

Goofy love. Twitterpation.
Awkward overbite love, braces
knobby knee headgear romance.
The best two weeks ever.

I would put mad miles on my
Huffy to sit with my first freckle
faced white girl who lived at
hop-skip jump address.

II.
Mom was cool and let it ride.
Our talk on interracial dating
would come later after the
inevitable ending.

But for now
there's Brooke's birthday party.
Me, the only boy invited
and five other
girls.

My ego does
the running man.

III.

There are two cars.

Her mother's station wagon and
daddy's Caprice Classic dark blue.

One packed with a giggling
crayola box of girls and room
for one more.

I am imagining
the smell of bullfrog sunscreen
mingling with juicy fruit gum.

There are two cars.
Her daddy suggests I ride
with him. *Just us fellas* he says.

There is one car.

IV.
We ride in silence.
Forty five minutes
of quiet. No warmth.
His eyes are bird
eggshell blue. Mouth
a tight sharp crease.
He watches the road
only. College ring
big as a billboard.
Red is pulsing
under his knuckle skin.
Something tight in
my chest unbinds
crawls up my throat
sits in my ear   tells me
not to make conversation.
We get there early. *Goddammit!*

No station wagon.

He won't unlock the door.
We sit. He won't look at me.
C'mon station wagon.
He pops the lock.

V.
I don't remember the
taste of the cake or the present
I wrapped myself.

I remember laughter.
The brown ebb and flow of the
lake shore.
My toes wiggling near
white ones in dark sand. I don't
remember how I get home.
I taste metal   hug Mama
throw up in the bathroom.

D&D: A Confession

After Junot Diaz's The Brief Wondrous
Life of Oscar Wao

I started rolling dice at the age of eleven.
On weekends, late into the night, I'd
blow into my buckeye brown tight fist
shake the bright red stones and let
them fly.

Surrounded by a crew of stone faced
white boys who'd survey my roll
with hopeful glances, I'd watch
the die twirl and settle,
check the numbers, then
proceed to slaughter. Open to
their bloodthirsty suggestions.

Dude, you're a third level
Elf Paladin. Use your broadsword
on the Orc battalion.

No way dude. If I want to wear
down their hit points I gotta
use my mace. Geez man I only
get one turn per round. And what
happens when it's their turn to attack?
I lost my enchanted shield to the Bugbear
a few turns ago, and all I have is this
chain mail, one flask of healing potion
and a prayer.

I hear you man. And we all
know how Orcs like to aim low.
I hope your hit points hold Bro.
If you die, I'll resurrect you, but
you'll have to give that cache of emeralds
in return.

I'd sip my Mr. Pibb
and munch on pretzels thoughtfully.
decisions, decisions.

Heavy is the lone black boy's head
in the world of Dungeons and Dragons.

Tisha (Record Press Play)

For The Once-Wallflower Poets

You would wind your waist
to the bassline.
Pop your body to the kick drum.
Work your arms in slow motion-
undulation like a hydra's heads.

We would watch you from
our wallflower patch positions
with kerosene imaginations
blazing blue.

We memorized
the words for you   only.
Every verse.
Your hips,
call and response.
Your breasts,
the bridge.

Later.
You would ask us to tell you who
sang what or
decipher that line Aaron Hall
crooned
while you were enveloped in
that slow drag butter churn grind
with Mr. Popular but not us.

We would watch.
Wishing for an out-of-body experience
to satiate the hunger that comes
from being there but not being   there.
We were the nappy headed, under-tall
scribes.

Closeted Dunbars
recording
remembering
rememory

feeding the place where poems are born

Remembering Bonita Applebum

Bonita Applebum be a
onyx colored
Milky Way sprinkled
infinity loop
of a goddess's laugh.

Bonita Applebum be
the pentatonic scale
squeezed into form fitting
denim overalls.

Bonita Applebum be
Coltrane's "Naima" at 88 bpms
riding an Ali Shaheed Muhummad break beat
bare back.

Bonita Applebum be your daddy's
woman before your mama came into the picture.

Bonita Applebum be leavin thugs
breathless, their eyes leaking water
from nostalgia.

Bonita Applebum's eyes shiny like
new vinyl, fresh like a Rudy Huxtable perm.

Bonita Applebum be your
first first.
First back porch
summer sunset French kiss,
first pack of Nag champa incense,
first hip-hop sample that makes you
seek out its source.

Bonita Applebum be
1989, baby dreads,
salt fish, ginger beer,
sweet iced tea, cassava,
kola champagne,
mud cloth, head wraps,
ashy knees, shea butter,
library cards, bottled water,
and rickety first time ancestor
shrines.

Bonita Applebum be black folks
in Birkenstocks   and that's okay.

Bonita Applebum's
bookshelf is bigger than yours.
What you gonna do about it?

Bonita Applebum be a dog eared
copy of *Erotic Noir*.

Bonita Applebum be light skinned
girl crushes on Lisa Bonet, Jasmine Guy,
Pebbles, and Tisha Campbell from *House Party*.

Bonita Applebum be dark skinned girl crushes on
Sheryl Lee Ralph, Eddie Murphy's first wife
from *Coming to America*, and Karyn White.

Bonita Applebum still knows the
lyrics to every song on Eric B. and Rakim's
Paid in Full album.

Bonita Applebum be your
first on purpose poke on the
dance floor.

Bonita Applebum be
the reason you got a Sankofa tattoo
on your left shoulder blade.

Bonita Applebum be
the rasp of Q-Tip's voice
that puts goose bumps on
your girl's neck even now.

Bonita Applebum
ain't 38-24-37 no more.

Bonita Applebum be
33 with a mortgage
and two degrees under her belt.
Your mama still asks about
Bonita
Bonita
Bonita?

Bonita Applebum be your
son's second grade teacher,
guidance counselor, Spanish tutor.

Bonita Applebum drives a
Toyota Forerunner, the hybrid model
with mud cloth seat covers.

Bonita Applebum is   still slamming
like a hip-hop song.

Ol' Man Strength

For Cornelius Eady

*"Sometimes you gotta find a way around those young
cats." —Cornelius Eady*

I.
Miles had to do it.
Toward the end, he only
peppered his tracks with
muted trumpet bursts.

Freddie Hubbard too.

You gotta realize he was an old geezer by then
and you gotta find your way around those young
cats,
that step into the game hungry, cocksure,
Looking for belts to take, starting spots.
Even Jordan did it.

Developed a post-up
spin-turn
jumper,
stutter step
off of the dribble pull-up,
that still caught Kobe off guard.
Drew a foul every time by
playing on youth's anxiousness.

II.

I almost fought an older
man over a woman,
once.

Stepped to him with
bare handed thunder and lightning
cursing.

I'm gonna kick yo' rusty ass!
You ain't my daddy!
Prove that shit then!!
He didn't even breathe hard
When he pulled out his .22.

I pulled out my deepest apologies.
Let the bass air out of my voice
like a punctured tire,
a shrieking deflating balloon.

Sir please forgive my trespass
My transgressions.
I meant no disrespect.
I'll be on my way, won't
Darken your door step.
Excuse me, My bad, Sir...
Mister Sir...

He found a way around
this young cat.

Red Giant

For Octavia Butler

She taught us to gaze.
To ponder the deepest reaches of our skin,
the nebula of our eyes.
Beyond beyond to the changeling within us
the extraterrestrials we are

the kindred tongues
spoken across time's continuum
the warmth of the blood that travels
wanders and pools. We will miss you
other Mother.

We chase your echo eagerly
into eternity's ether.

White Dwarf

For Octavia Butler

On the roof after
word of your sudden passing
I watch the stars dim

Slow Fade

For James "J-Dilla" Yancey

"Transition with a real slow fade"
—Erykah Badu, "Telephone"

Scratch hiss.

Crisp and needle sharp.
This is your life on vinyl.

Your ear has the forty-niner's intuition
for black gold spooled and disc shaped.

Your heart is a divining rod.
You, resurrector of bpms.

You
kept digging.

Since you left
what you've known of hip-hop is over.

Its all repetitive keys
greased stripper poles
and choruses.

There are no more breaks.

Just dumb tongues forsaking
to suckle from soul.

Momma always said getting it natural
was better than formula.

Son of Motown

Minister of the head nod

Encoder of hypnotic soulquarian drums

Seamless tailor of the beat match
with blends so tight you never caught
the progression to the next song.

Low End Theory practioner
all you felt was the bottom.

Forerunner
your beats still called exclusive
even after Lupus started its
slow fade through your body.

Who else can hold the claim
of finishing an album
from their death bed?

I imagine,
as your heart hiccuped
an epilogue

you   drumming out a beat
with your gaunt fingers.

Head bowed
your slip cover body rippling
with kick-drum, snare,
your brain, caught in a stubborn loop
willed your hands to sound out breaths
slap skin to ignored dinner tray
cafeteria table style

as your mother
recorded at your bedside
she   the butterfly net
catching the last of
your winged light before
the next transition

Malcolm X's Glasses Speak

The Minister's eyes
were weak but hungry
like a newborn's
voracious O of a mouth.

When he placed me on
his face for the first time
I felt the ultra violet
hum of his gaze pass through me.

Then and there I knew
my purpose. He would
never miss a word, never
under my watch.

We knew every book
of the prison library
by touch, smell, print
size, font.

All I've witnessed could
not fit snugly into Alex Haley's
book. There is not enough ink.
His typewriter gears would

ruin from over work. I rested
when the Minister rested. He'd remove
me only   to sleep   put me on
only after Saalat.

I've seen skeptics wilt
under his stare. Watched
the white reporters adams apples
bob then rise as he spoke truth to power.

I will never forget the handshake
he shared with King. So firm,
hands calloused very much like the Minister's.
His eyes   so much older

than we assumed. If only we could have
sat a while. Spoke longer. Ah.
Sister Betty, skin, the color of
Ethiopian coffee. Strong like it too.

The girls, tiny testaments to
their shared loving. What
more to reveal? He was
always cleaning my lenses.

As if he could not believe
what he was seeing. Such
wickedness, the poverty, he
went where the talking heads wouldn't dare.

I was his steadfast ally
when his ears betrayed him
and the tailing began.
I helped the Minister see

what was on the crest
of this next becoming.
When he was felled
I caught Betty's tears.

Helped him focus on the
angel to his right furiously
recording this moment.
As his light faded from my lenses

like a white dwarf star.
Yuri Kochiyama folded
me neat and quiet in her lap
wiped away the blood and
handed me to Betty

in the quick and quiet moments
between the pulse and pound
of shock and grief.

Bell Canto

For Sean Bell and Family

Your mind wants to believe
it was a misunderstanding.

The officers were scared rookies.
It was dark.

But truth suffers no allowances.

Spread out before you are snatches of
eye-witness accounts in print. The grainy footage
of gun butts tempering jaws; the swollen voice of
the fiancée.

This is a different type of jilting; no story
of a runaway bride found with thawing feet,
and no sign of her imagined Latino abductor.

No. You don't want to believe this.
Your mind is tired of "Again"

This happens.
Same city.
Same sons.
Same make and model.
Same implied threat empty hands carry.
Same text book response.
Same salvo.
Same torrential rain of shell casings

muting a Bell.

Clip emptied.

Reload

Your mind is a busted reel
of images; that officer from grade school
who never wore his gun around the students.

Reload

The stories you ghosted
from the barber's chair;
regulation choke holds
boot heels on testicles
a nightstick renovating a ribcage

Reload

The white boy in 10th grade
who caught a cafeteria tray to the head
for Rodney King in '92

The forearm planted in
your chest from the
officer who didn't
care to hear your explanation
for arriving late to a sold out
ball game even though you
bought tickets in advance.

His words
"No admittance"
mean more now than then.

You use this as your caption
to narrate the picture
of the uniformed triggermen in the photo
silent unblinking
hands hidden
behind their backs
at ease
acquitted.

Your mind wants for a
parable, a moral
and there isn't one.

Richard Pryor Haiku

Richard Pryor's laugh
Wet razor under tongue
of Legba's hot mouth

Snagglepuss Spills His Guts on
E! True Hollywood Story

The Pink Panther!?
Fuck him!

Always this calm quiet
androgynous cool on the exterior.

But if you let me tell it
he always stayed on both sides of the fence.
If you catch my drift.

Kept quiet. Never said a word
unless it was absolutely necessary.
Just strolled around and winked a lot
ashing those long thin French cigarettes.

He's the one that got the prize I guess.
Worldwide film exposure, those Corning
insulation commercials, the string of films.

That bubblegum colored pussy-foot
never acknowledged what he was.
Conveniently forgot our quiet dinners
in Jellystone Park.

We'd stroll through the forest
dine on delicate pheasants together.
Feed giblet gravy to each other.
And for dessert I'd mount him
just like he'd ask me to.

Oh Snagglepuss you're so gentle
he'd purr in his bass-line voice.
Damn that Bazooka Joe colored bastard!

How many times? How many times
did I put my career on hold for him?

You think I liked schlepping around
with those Hanna-Barbara flunkies!?

Puh-leeze! I was a Stanislavsky Method
actor thank you very much.
Yogi and Boo-Boo were vaudeville shams.
Huckleberry Hound was a chitlin' circuit regular.

Some say he even wore blackface.
Did a couple of minstrel shows once.
I'm not surprised. He did roll tight
with ol' Bugs Bunny. And we all know
he had no problem rubbing on a little
boot polish on his face. But I digress.

When the big money came calling
Ol' Pinky packed his bags and gave
me some song and dance about how
I'd never have to work again once he got big.
No more anvils, no more falling boulders.

No more exit   stage right.

But I should have known.
After the films, the accolades,
and his Blake Edwards endorsements
my phone stopped ringing. No more
pleasantries and pheasants no more
grooming each others pink fur
with our tongues.

Snaggle Poo. He told me
the last time we were together
it just won't work things are
different now. I have different
priorities. I run with a different crowd.
You know the business.

This isn't Jellystone. People talk.
You were great but from this point
on I can't be seen with you.
You know you're… a little more open
with your gestures, and then its your voice.

People know right away what you are, but
me… well, Olive Oyl thinks I'm a man's man anyway.
Besides she says I'm much more
understanding than that one-eyed
sailor cat.

But hey babe that's the
way of the business
see you in the funny papers.

So now you see why I never stay
on screen too long. Heavens to
Murgatroyd it still hurts even! So
just realize that whenever I exit
stage right its not for laughs,
I just don't want anyone to
see me cry.

On Watching Black Poets Dance at the AWP Closing Party

We were mahogany electrons
arms flight ready
see-sawing shoulders
hydraulic lifted hips
dark matter particles
crunked into a matrix

faces cast in groove grind
grin of ecstasy.
We were syrupy reeds
chopped and screwed
swimming in a wake
of indigo throb

Beyond us   the crowd
struggled to stay
current
fighting the low end theory
their limbs couldn't capture

To Be Published

do I write of flora to cull interest?
Write of loam and budding?
Of chrysanthemums, tulips, brilliant and bursting?
Or of petals the color of raging corpuscles
that take the hilltop of cheeks flushed from surprise?
How would I describe that rich fertile earth
which holds the color of me, that colors my poems?
Would convenient omission of such darker tones
permit me entrance?

O' Bards how should I fix my poem's
mouth? What light words should
ebb from thick lips? How slender the
words? How flat? How flaccid? To lie upon
your pages?

Angels with Angles

Dedicated to William Edmonson's "Angel" sculpture

After lookin at mine they say
Angels is supposed to be pretty.
Should have gossamer wings and all
with light shining out all about
their lovely heads like slices
of good morning sun. Type of
light that makes your eyes tear up
and run over like if you left
the tub running.

Church folk say blessings come
like that. My angel come from
the cornerstone of a long gone bank.
Its wings are a limestone slab from
a Masonic temple. Its body—thick
like the skin on my hands—was
cleaved from a home going marker
I carved out years ago. My angel
is pretty sittin all hushed and cool

so you can hear the air sing
around its smooth head. Ask me
where I found it and I'll tell you
seek and ye shall find. Cause God
give it to me, *like he give me the*
mind and the hand I suppose,[1]

---

[1] Edmonson quote; "William Edmonson a Primitive Sculptor." *New York Times*, February 10, 1951.

and pretty angels is every where.
Some just waiting on a hammer
and chisel to free 'em.

For the Unkissed and Suitors

Dedicated to a segment of Chris Ofili's "Afro Muses"
Portrait Series

I.
It's an off the shoulder
bare skinned black
burnt pecan coloured love
we yield to. No matter
how frightening, despite
the unknown nappiness
and amount of kink,
we still advance hissing
like hot combs and serpents
shedding self consciousness
skins. Emerging in glistening prism
chrysalis coloured dashikis.

This is for the unkissed,
the bejeweled portrait princesses
waiting at a moments word
for that ecru, sepia toned, azure
tinted touch, press of flesh
on earlobe, cheek back bone
nape of neck.

II.
This is for the suitors
clothed in starbursts
and indigo supernovas.
Their afros exploded sunspots.

Beards   begotten of Baraka and
Castro clipped strong backs, strong chin profile,
eyes a Roy Ayers song "Searching"
seeking to be suited frame by frame.

Ajar

Flicker

For MKL

The body never forgets.
Muscle memory they call it.

The last time we kissed
a few weeks into the new year
three years ago
could have been then.

In the warmth of
your car   my hands
remembered where
to smooth

where
to tuck
how to pull you close.

The joy of the rememory
brought back our choreography
of loving

how you curved
against me
how we fit so well
I called you puzzle
piece

Your lips

the best
reminder of the good times

Your tongue
a ghostwriter's limb
with conjure strokes

Your name
an incantation
I mouth now and then
wishing us back
in your car
flickering
on.

Outstretched

Guide my hands to find those
soft places that need touch.
I am a man and a slave to
the general understanding that
we must make the first move.

But I need to tell you. Let
you know there are times
I'm unsure   cannot capture
hints or glimpses of unspoken
want behind your eyes.

Maybe a brick with a note
may do the trick. Sugar
smash me one good time against
forgetting and be my guide.
I place my hands in yours   this time

You take the lead. My uncertainties
would melt away from the heat of
need in your fingers. Lead me where
you wish me to settle and be certain
I will follow each direction like a blind man
who puts his faith in the outstretched.

Misdirected

A Bop in the Key of Quest

*Sampled Elements: "Find a Way" from A Tribe Called
Quest's* Love Movement *album.*

"The whole world see it but you can't" —Q-Tip

"Tell me what you want, what you really really want!"
—The Spice Girls

How you gonna walk in here
all smiles and sugar water?
How you gonna distract me
from my work smelling all
freshly picked? You, with them
horn of Africa curves and all;
making me want to learn a new language,
thank your mother, piss off your father,
take your last name, call in sick.

So you've caught my heart for the evening.

Momma says man's failing
is his misdirected multi tasking.
He only has two arms but swears
he can juggle women times ten.
I know my limits, but still I end up
like that Aesop fable dog.
The one who lost his only bone
to a river reflection.

Yes, sometimes
greed has greased my need.
But what's a man to do?

In my line of work every day
is a silk road caravan of lovely.
Seems like my focus is
as transient as this city.
And here you are,
a tempting dare, making that line
between friendship and the physical
a fading sunset.

We whisper warnings in between
the smack and suck of hungry skin
but can't hear above the traffic of
this ripened moment.

Kissed my cheek moved in you've confused things

How does a jog become a sprint?
I'm still wishing for a marathon
and there you go elsewhere.
Dropping that one word that turns
possibility to porridge. Friendship.

I'm anchored to this moment.
Your about-face, far quicker than
a boxcutter's slice.

I'm the one crumbled and here you come.
With them horn of Africa curves and all;
making me want to learn a new language,
thank your mother, piss off your father,
take your last name, call in sick.

So you've caught my heart for the evening
Kissed my cheek moved in you've confused things
Should I just sit out or come harder?
Help me find my way.

Reciprocation

After Dennis Brutus's "Carnality"

Ah the promise of flesh
The shock of a tongue wandering.
The smooth belly spotted with sweat.
All have commandments
to follow, study, to show thy self approved.
Hallelujahs and hosannas   do unto others
as you would have them do unto you.

Brownku 2

sweat in her navel
her hands commandments
go south young man

In the Car

Derrick are you single?

Yeah.

(pregnant silence)

Soooooo.
What about you? Are you single?

Yes. I'm single.

(silence as thick as thieves during a blackout)

[Running ticker tape dialogue in my head]

Issheaskingcauseshe'sinterestedorissheasking
justtoaskwhojustasksjusttoaskwhatdoIsaynow
turnupthemusic NO turndownthemusicsaysomething
WaitIhaven'tsaidanythingyet OH NO Igottosaysomething
becoolbecoolICECOLD! Relaxawwdaaamnmylipsaregoing
drydon'tclamupyouchappedlipbastastardsaysomething!!!!

Really? Word. Ok.

Couched (the last of the summer poems) for...

On your couch
we rocked like
two rain-slicked
brown birch trees.

Bare backed
my hands sculpt your
thighs in
to
a hungry   Y.

Dating Koan #1

If I arrive and you are there
but he's still there
in every way but body
what is the meaning of travel?

Recipe for Putting a Lover to Sleep

For NM

You will need a candle. Preferably a scented one. Make it lavender, eucalyptus, or both. Gather your fresh sheets. Sprinkle baby powder on the bare mattress. Make sure the sheets are cool if its summer or piping hot to the touch fresh from the dryer if its winter. Spread the mattress cover taut and wide. Let the ends hug the corners tightly like you hold her in quiet places. Whip the top sheet into the air. Watch it bloom then billow and float down like a lofty exhale. Next comes the comforter. Remember you are its namesake. Tonight make sure it covers the bed like a canopy. Flip all pillows to their cool sides so they ease the breathing upon impact. Curve them so they caress her cheekbones like your own warm palm. Stand back and survey your craft. Turn the bed down. Leave a space where sheet and blanket form a border. Light the candle. Snuff the lights. Call for her. If she doesn't answer, pad lightly down the hallway. If you find her dozing on the couch your task is that much easier. Lay your hand on her shoulder. If she is a light sleeper this is all you need to do. If she is a heavy one rock her till her eyes flutter open and focus on you and warm like just lit amber lanterns. Guide her to the bedroom. The candle's scent will tug her in like an anxious lover. Pull back comforter blanket sheet fold each slowly over her lower case s shaped form. Say nothing. When she rolls onto her stomach rub her back counter clockwise. Hum if you'd like or let the playback of your hand's looped hiss on the turntable of her skin repeat like a record's last dusty groove. Match each rub to her inhale, exhale. Wait for the intermission of tension as stress vacates her body. Slow the loop to heartbeat pace. Blow out the candle.

Haibun on Transition

So good. The beginnings are always so good. Her head on my shoulder.
Grocery shopping. Listening to her and then showing her how well I've listened. Prolonged good nights. Her asking me to stay was the best, me asking her
to come over was better. Being her pillow, her comforter.

Scented candles
Fresh pies cool on counter top
Music in the kitchen

This is a lesson. I have to tell myself this is a lesson.
I'm a practicing Buddhist and I'm trying to understand the philosophy of letting go and the freedom of being desire free. But there's something to be said for desire. Desire feeds the poem. It feeds the pen, makes the muscle coax the bones to testify.
Like I said, I'm a "practicing" Buddhist.

My brown clenched fingers
Aftertaste of want
Unfolded lotus

We were driving in silence. I hate silence, especially
when there's something that needs to be said, but isn't
and it sits between us like a looming cloud covered mountain.

Tires on asphalt
Hollow rattle of manhole
Raindrops drum a dirge

Carry-Out

For KJ

Once it was all more than this.

5 dvds aligned neatly
in a large brown paper bag.

One pair of felt boots
tucked into place.

Our eyes meet briefly
during the hand off.

We exchange
sentences.

The bag rustles
in passing.

If people were
watching us

they would think this
moment a purchase.

A pick-up of a take-out order
called in.

Poem about running into you on the street after not seeing you for a while.

Seeing you
after all this time
reveals to me two things.

One.
Your flame has diminished considerably.

Two.
I'm a different moth now.

Sourpatch Kiss

"Everyone is in love, except you…"
Bob Holman, "Night Fears"

The first time I tried to write
this poem, I tried to make it
all deep and introspective.
But I scratched that idea 'cause
I don't want to be deep and
introspective. I like my feelings
freshly dug up with the soft
dark earthy smell still on 'em.

Then I tried to be brief,
and struggled to think
of a one-liner with dry humor
that makes me seem more
sophisticated than I really am.

Then I went for the tear
jerker poem, but I scratched
that idea in the end and I
don't want pity cause I'm
no where near pitiful. And this
poem ain't about heart break
so much as it is about longing.

I think what I want
is a plain poem that
doesn't come off as
pleading prose

or a poet's quiet cry for
help   hidden in a bushel
of loaded metaphors.

But I'm not mad either
or bitter at my romantic
state of affairs. Its just that
I need, y'know?

The Jesus Age

They say at this age
I have two options.

Walk on water
or be crucified.

I laugh at this.

Their mouths
are Mona Lisa's.

Their eyes are set
serious
still as the Dead Sea.

"The Sweet Home Men Series"
Is a continuing series of persona poems in the voices of the enslaved men of the Sweet Home plantation from Toni Morrison's Pulitzer Prize winning novel *Beloved*, specifically, Halle, Paul F, Paul A, Sixo, and Paul D. *"One crazy, one sold, one missing, one burnt and me, licking iron, with my hands crossed behind me."* —Paul D

"Thirty Mile Woman: Sixo's Song"
"Tubob" or "Tubab" is an African term for either a "foreigner" or in some cases "white man." It is disputed whether it is a derogatory term or not.

"What I'm Told: Paul D's Origin"
A veil or caul is a full face mask which may be sometimes found covering the face of a child at birth. Such births are rare and hold special significance for the child born in such a manner. Many belief systems hold that being born with a veil is a sign of special destiny and psychic abilities, or good luck.

"Paul A to Paul D Eintou"
The "Eintou" is an African American poetic form that consists of seven lines with a syllabic word count for each line; 2-4-6-8-6-4-2. Eintou is a West African term for pearl as in "pearl of wisdom." Visually, the shape of the poem itself can bear resemblance to a pearl.

"Halle Tells How They Broke Him"
"Clabber" is a food produced by allowing unpasteurized milk to turn sour at a specific humidity and temperature. Over time the milk thickens or curdles into a yogurt-like substance with a strong, sour flavor. In rural areas of the Southern United States, it was commonly eaten for breakfast with brown sugar, nutmeg,

cinnamon, or molasses added. Some people also eat it with fruit or black pepper and cream.

"Color Commentary"

"Timheri International" is a small nightclub located in the Northwest corridor of Washington, D.C., in the neighborhood of Adams Morgan. The author has frequented it from time to time.

"K St. Lunch Hour Tanka"

"Tanka" are 31-syllable poems. As a form of poetry, tanka poems evoke a moment or mark an occasion with concision and musicality. In Japanese, tanka is often written in one straight line, but in English and other languages, the lines are usually divided into the five syllabic units: 5-7-5-7-7.

"Brownku"

The author's variation on the Japanese short form of haiku.

"Kitchen Gods"

"Adinkra" are visual symbols, originally created by the Akan of Ghana and the Gyaman of Côte d'Ivoire in West Africa that represent concepts or aphorisms. "Cerulean" is a shade of blue. "Hoppin' John" is the Southern United States' version of the rice and beans dish traditional throughout West Africa. It consists of black-eyed peas (or field peas) and rice, with chopped onion and sliced bacon, seasoned with a bit of salt.

An "**earman**" is known as a musician who plays specifically by ear and has the ability to pick up tunes and arrangements on the fly.

"Gust"

Hurricane Hugo was a destructive Category 5 hurricane that struck Guadeloupe, Montserrat, St. Croix, Puerto Rico, Antigua, North and South Carolina in September of the 1989 Atlantic hurricane season.

"Remembering Bonita Applebum"
"Bonita Applebum" was a popular single from A Tribe Called Quest's debut album *People's Instinctive Travels and the Paths of Rhythm*. A hip-hop classic.

"Slow Fade"
James Dewitt Yancey, better known by the stage names J Dilla and Jay Dee, was a hip-hop record producer who emerged from the mid-1990s underground hip-hop scene in Detroit, Michigan. He is known as one of the most innovative producers of his generation, most notably for the production of critically acclaimed albums by Common, Busta Rhymes, A Tribe Called Quest, and The Pharcyde. He was a member of Slum Village and produced their acclaimed debut album, *Fan-Tas-Tic (Vol. 1)* and their follow-up, *Fantastic, Vol. 2*. He died after a long battle with Lupus, three days after his thirty-second birthday. Hip-hop legend tells that he completed two solo albums *Donuts* and *The Shining* in the hospital, from his death bed.

"Dating Koan #1"
A koan is a fundamental part of the history and lore of Zen Buddhism. It consists of a story, dialogue, question, or statement; the meaning of which cannot be understood by rational thinking, yet it may be accessible by intuition. One widely known koan is "Two hands clap and there is a sound; what is the sound of one hand clapping?"

"Haibun on Transition"
A haibun is a literary composition that combines prose and haiku. The range of haibun is broad and includes, but is not limited to, the following forms of prose: autobiography, biography, diary, essay, historiography, prose poem, short story, and travel literature.

About the Author

Derrick Weston Brown holds an MFA in creative writing, from American University. He has studied poetry under Dr. Tony Medina at Howard University and Cornelius Eady at American University. He is a graduate of the Cave Canem Summer workshop for black poets and the VONA summer workshop. His work has appeared in such literary journals as *Warpland, Mythium, Ginsoko, DrumVoices, The Columbia Poetry Review*, and the online journals *Capital Beltway*, Howard University's *Amistad, LocusPoint*, and *MiPOesias*. He works as a bookseller and book buyer for a wonderful bookstore which is operated by the nonprofit Teaching For Change, and is located within the restaurant, bar, coffee shop, and performance space known as Busboys and Poets. As the first Poet-In-Residence of Busboys and Poets, he is the founder and curator of **The Nine on the Ninth**, a five-year-old monthly poetry series, and helps coordinate the poetry programming at the 14th & V Streets location. He teaches poetry and creative writing to an amazing crew of seventh and eighth graders at Hart Middle school in Southeast Washington, D.C., as part of the D.C. Creative Writing Workshop. He is a native of Charlotte, North Carolina, and resides in Mount Rainier, Maryland. *Wisdom Teeth* is his first collection of poetry.

Busboys and Poets Press is a subsidiary of Busboys and Poets, a restaurant and community resource center for artists, activists, writers, thinkers, and dreamers who believe that a better world is possible.

Busboys and Poets
2121 14th St. NW
Washington, DC 20009
www.busboysandpoets.com

PM Press was founded at the end of 2007 by a small collection of folks with decades of publishing, media, and organizing experience. PM Press co-conspirators have published and distributed hundreds of books, pamphlets, CDs, and DVDs. Members of PM have founded enduring book fairs, spearheaded victorious tenant organizing campaigns, and worked closely with bookstores, academic conferences, and even rock bands to deliver political and challenging ideas to all walks of life. We're old enough to know what we're doing and young enough to know what's at stake.

We seek to create radical and stimulating fiction and non-fiction books, pamphlets, t-shirts, visual and audio materials to entertain, educate, and inspire you. We aim to distribute these through every available channel with every available technology, whether that means you are seeing anarchist classics at our bookfair stalls; reading our latest vegan cookbook at the café; downloading geeky fiction e-books; or digging new music and timely videos from our website.

PM Press is always on the lookout for talented and skilled volunteers, artists, activists and writers to work with. If you have a great idea for a project or can contribute in some way, please get in touch.

PM Press
PO Box 23912
Oakland, CA 94623
www.pmpress.org

FRIENDS OF PM

These are indisputably momentous times—the financial system is melting down globally and the Empire is stumbling. Now more than ever there is a vital need for radical ideas.

In the three years since its founding—and on a mere shoestring—PM Press has risen to the formidable challenge of publishing and distributing knowledge and entertainment for the struggles ahead. With over 100 releases to date, we have published an impressive and stimulating array of literature, art, music, politics, and culture. Using every available medium, we've succeeded in connecting those hungry for ideas and information to those putting them into practice.

Friends of PM allows you to directly help impact, amplify, and revitalize the discourse and actions of radical writers, filmmakers, and artists. It provides us with a stable foundation from which we can build upon our early successes and provides a much-needed subsidy for the materials that can't necessarily pay their own way. You can help make that happen—and receive every new title automatically delivered to your door once a month—by joining as a Friend of PM Press. And, we'll throw in a free t-shirt when you sign up.

Here are your options:

- $25 a month: Get all books and pamphlets plus 50% discount on all webstore purchases
- $25 a month: Get all CDs and DVDs plus 50% discount on all webstore purchases
- $40 a month: Get all PM Press releases plus 50% discount on all webstore purchases
- $100 a month: Superstar—Everything plus PM merchandise, free downloads, and 50% discount on all webstore purchases

For those who can't afford $25 or more a month, we're introducing Sustainer Rates at $15, $10, and $5. Sustainers get a free PM Press t-shirt and a 50% discount on all purchases from our website.

Your Visa or Mastercard will be billed once a month, until you tell us to stop. Or until our efforts succeed in bringing the revolution around. Or the financial meltdown of Capital makes plastic redundant. Whichever comes first.

Also from Busboys and Poets Press/ PM Press

Suspended Somewhere Between:
A Book of Verse
Akbar Ahmed
$15.95
ISBN: 978-1-60486-485-4

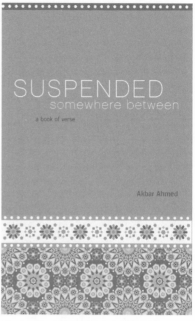

Akbar Ahmed's *Suspended Somewhere Between* is a collection of poetry from the man the BBC calls "the world's leading authority on contemporary Islam." A mosaic of Ahmed's life, which has traversed cultural and religious barriers, this book of verse is personal with a vocal range from introspective and reflective to romantic and emotive to historical and political. The poems take the reader from the forbidding valleys and mountains of Waziristan in the tribal areas of Pakistan to the think tanks and halls of power in Washington, D.C.; from the rustic tranquility of Cambridge to the urban chaos of Karachi.

The collection spans half a century of writing and gives the reader a front row seat to the drama of a world in turmoil. Can there be more drama than Ahmed's first memories as a boy of four on a train through the killing fields of North India during the partition of the subcontinent in 1947? Or the breakup of Pakistan into two counties amidst mass violence in 1971? Yet, in the midst of change and uncertainty, there is the optimism and faith of a man with confidence in his fellow man and in the future, despite the knowledge that perhaps the problems and challenges of the changing world would prove to be too great.

Ahmed's poetry was a constant source of solace and renewal to which he escaped for inspiration and sanity. He loved poetry of every kind whether English, Urdu, or Persian. Ahmed was as fascinated by Keats and Coleridge as he was by Rumi and Ghalib. For us, he serves as a guide to the inner recesses of the Muslim world showing us its very heart. Through the poems, the reader gets fresh insights into the Muslim world and its struggles. Above all, they carry the eternal message of hope and compassion.

ALSO FROM BUSBOYS AND POETS PRESS/ PM PRESS

The 5th Inning
E. Ethelbert Miller
$18.95
ISBN: 978-1-60486-062-7

The 5th Inning is poet and literary activist E. Ethelbert Miller's second memoir. Coming after *Fathering Words: The Making of an African American Writer* (published in 2000), this book finds Miller returning to baseball, the game of his youth, in order to find the metaphor that will provide the measurement of his life. Almost 60, he ponders whether his life can now be entered into the official record books as a success or failure.

The 5th Inning is one man's examination of personal relationships, depression, love and loss. This is a story of the individual alone on the pitching mound or in the batters box. It's a box score filled with remembrance. It's a combination of baseball and the blues.

About the Author:

E. Ethelbert Miller is a literary activist. He is board chair of the Institute for Policy Studies (IPS). He is also a board member of The Writer's Center and editor of *Poet Lore* magazine. The author of several collections of poems, his last book *How We Sleep On The Nights We Don't Make Love* (Curbstone Press, 2004) was an Independent Publisher Award Finalist. Miller received the 1995 O.B. Hardison Jr. Poetry Prize. He was awarded in 1996 an honorary doctorate of literature from Emory & Henry College. In 2003 his memoir *Fathering Words: The Making of An African American Writer* (St. Martin's Press, 2000) was selected by the D.C. WE READ for its one book, one city program sponsored by the D.C. Public Libraries. In 2004 Miller was awarded a Fulbright to visit Israel. *Poets & Writers* presented him with the 2007 Barnes & Noble/Writers for Writers Award. Mr. Miller is often heard on National Public Radio (NPR).